6 american popular piano

REPERTOIRE

Compositions by
Christopher Norton

Additional Compositions
and Arrangements
Dr. Scott McBride Smith

Editor
Dr. Scott McBride Smith

Associate Editor
Clarke MacIntosh

Book Design & Engraving
Andrew Jones

T0056474

Cover Design
Wagner Design

A Note about this Book

Pop music styles can be grouped into three broad categories:

- **lyrical** — pieces with a beautiful singing quality and rich harmonies; usually played at a slow tempo;
- **rhythmic** — more up-tempo pieces, with energetic, catchy rhythms; these often have a driving left hand part;
- **ensemble** — works meant to be played with other musicians, or with backing tracks (or both!); this type of piece requires careful listening and shared energy.

American Popular Piano has been deliberately designed to develop skills in all three areas.

You can integrate the cool, motivating pieces in **American Popular Piano** into your piano studies in several ways.

- pick a piece you like and learn it; when you're done, pick another!
- choose a piece from each category to develop a complete range of skills in your playing;
- polish a particular favorite for your local festival or competition. Works from **American Popular Piano** are featured on the lists of required pieces for many festivals and competitions;
- use the pieces as optional contemporary selections in music examinations;
- Or...just have fun!

Going hand-in-hand with the repertoire in **American Popular Piano** are the innovative **Etudes Albums** and **Skills Books**, designed to enhance each student's musical experience by building technical and aural skills.

- **Technical Etudes** in both Classical and Pop Styles are based on musical ideas and technical challenges drawn from the repertoire. Practice these to improve your chops!
- **Improvisation Etudes** offer an exciting new approach to improvisation that guides students effortlessly into spontaneous creativity. Not only does the user-friendly module structure integrate smoothly into traditional lessons, it opens up a whole new understanding of the repertoire being studied.
- **Skills Books** help students develop key supporting skills in sight-reading, ear-training and technique; presented in complementary study modules that are both practical and effective.

Use all of the elements of **American Popular Piano** together to incorporate a comprehensive course of study into your everyday routine. The carefully thought-out pacing makes learning almost effortless. Making music and real progress has never been so much fun!

Library and Archives Canada Cataloguing in Publication

Norton, Christopher, 1953-

American popular piano [music] : repertoire / compositions by Christopher Norton ;
additional compositions and arrangements, Scott McBride Smith ;
editor, Scott McBride Smith ; associate editor, Clarke MacIntosh.

To be complete in 11 volumes.
Compact disc inserted on p. [3] of each v. contains instrumental backings for ensemble repertoire and improvisation études.
Publisher's nos.: APP R-00 (level P); APP R-01 (level 1); APP R-02 (level 2); APP R-03 (level 3); APP R-04 (level 4); APP R-05 (level 5).
Contents: Level P -- Level 1 -- Level 2 -- Level 3 -- Level 4 -- Level 5.
Miscellaneous information: The series is organized in 11 levels, from preparatory to level 10, each including a repertoire album, an etudes album, a skills book, a "technic" book, and an instrumental backings compact disc.

ISBN 1-897379-00-5 (level P).--ISBN 1-897379-01-3 (level 1).--ISBN 1-897379-02-1 (level 2).--ISBN 1-897379-03-X (level 3).--
ISBN 1-897379-04-8 (level 4).--ISBN 1-897379-05-6 (level 5).--ISBN 978-1-897379-00-4 (level P).--ISBN 978-1-897379-01-1 (level 1).--
ISBN 978-1-897379-02-8 (level 2).--ISBN 978-1-897379-03-5 (level 3).--ISBN 978-1-897379-04-2 (level 4).--ISBN 978-1-897379-05-9 (level 5).--
ISBN 978-1-897379-06-6 (level 6).--ISBN 978-1-897379-07-3 (level 7).--ISBN 978-1-897379-08-0 (level 8)

1. Piano music--Teaching pieces. I. Smith, Scott McBride II. MacIntosh, S. Clarke, 1959- III. Title. IV. Title: Repertoire

MT222.N883 2006   786.2   C2006-906213-7

LEVEL 6 REPERTOIRE
Table of Contents

Summer Sunday Afternoon

Christopher Norton

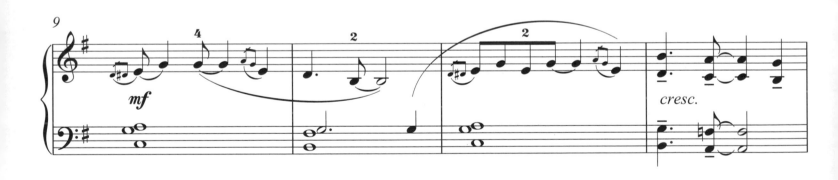

Out On The Plain

Christopher Norton

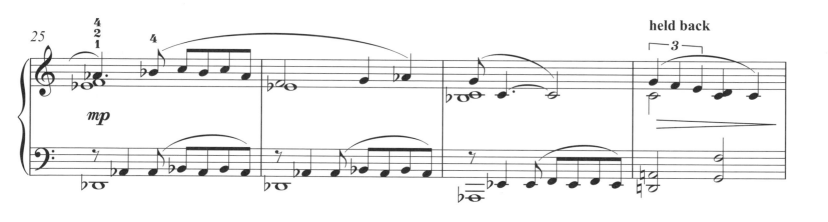

6

con ped.

A Light Touch

Christopher Norton

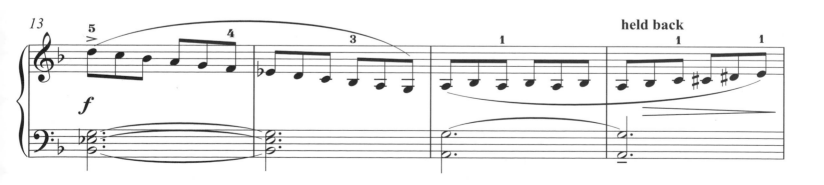

8

Autumn Stroll

Christopher Norton

Timeless

Christopher Norton

In the Desert

Christopher Norton

Slightly slowing **Poco a tempo**

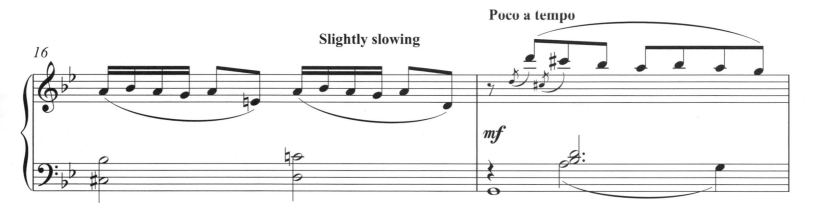

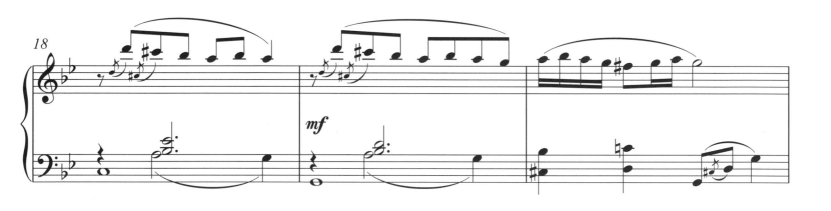

Slowing **Slower still**

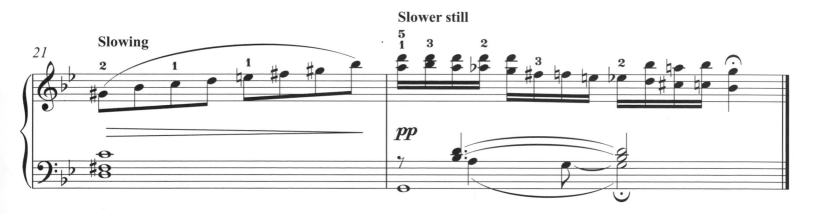

To the Stars

Christopher Norton

Tragedy

Christopher Norton

Light on My Feet

Christopher Norton

With humor ♩ = 96-108
swung 8ths

Heavy Footed

Christopher Norton

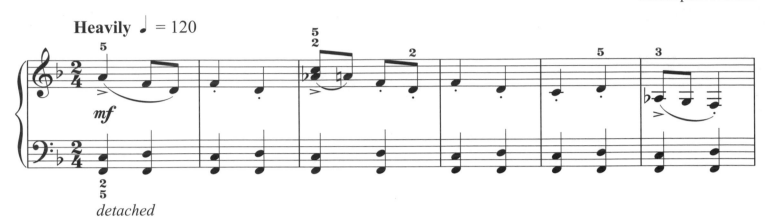

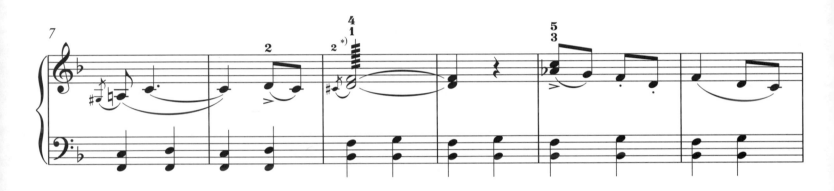

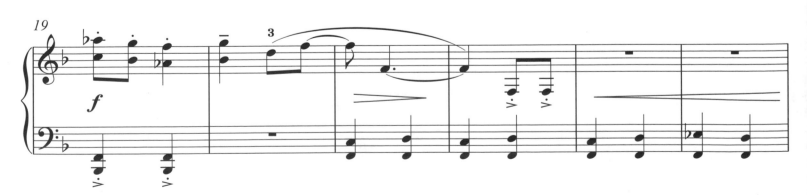

*) Alternate between the notes as fast as you can.

Latin Promenade

Christopher Norton

Illyrian Dance

Christopher Norton

Boxed In

Christopher Norton

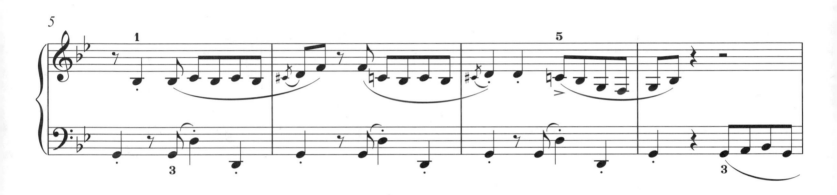

Subdivided

Christopher Norton

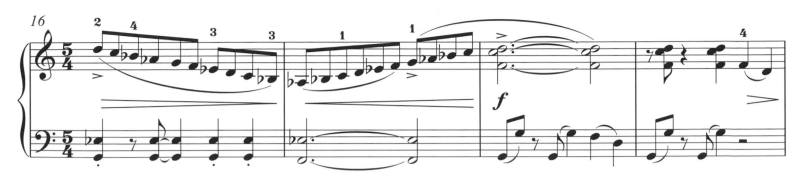

Fiddle Tune

Christopher Norton

Fireman's Boogie

Christopher Norton

Fiery ♩ = 116

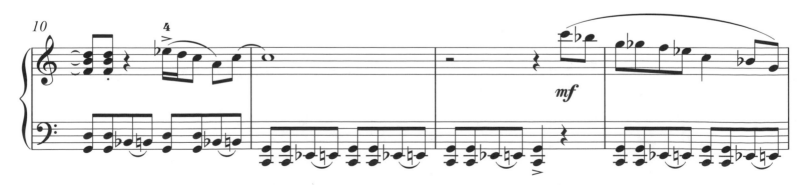

Bowling Green

Christopher Norton

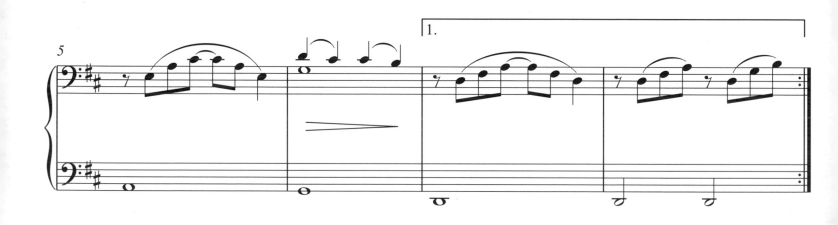

PIANO SOLO

Bowling Green

Christopher Norton

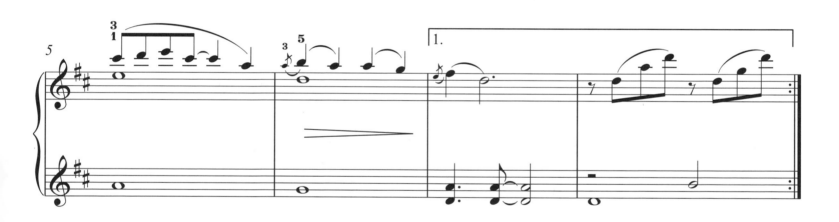

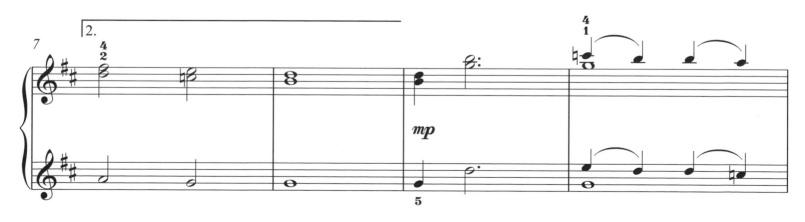

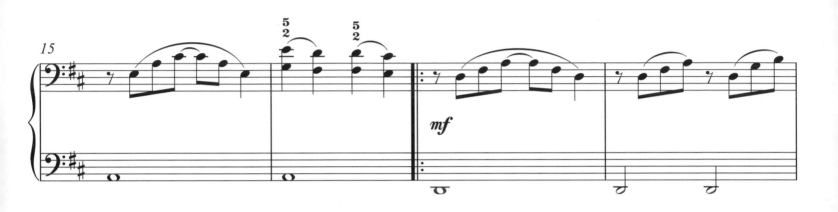

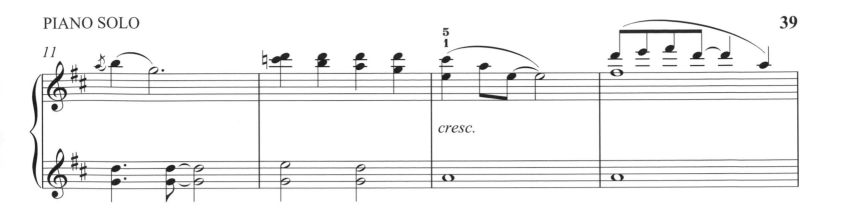

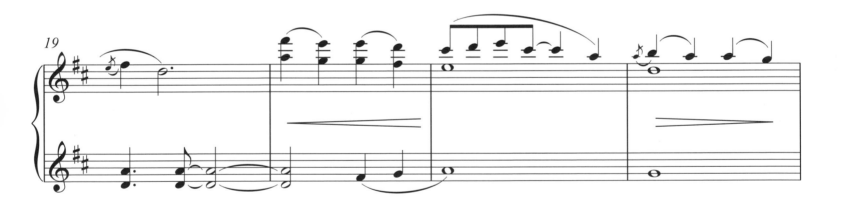

Clean Sweep

Christopher Norton

Clean Sweep

Christopher Norton

With energy ♩ = 120

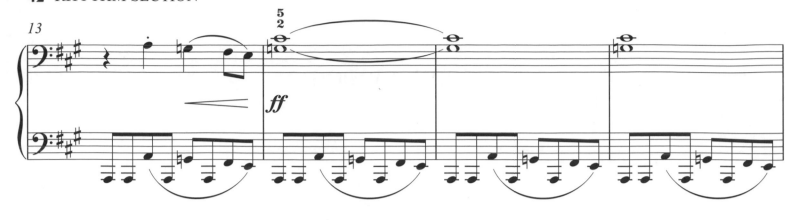

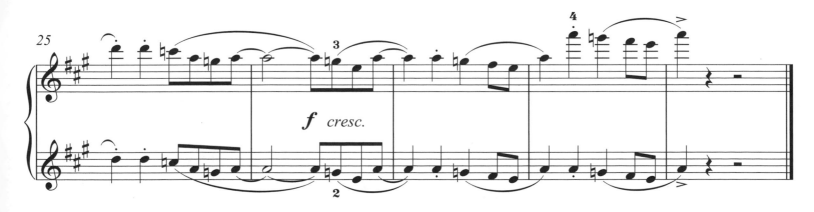

The Knights Prepare

Christopher Norton

PIANO SOLO

The Knights Prepare

Christopher Norton

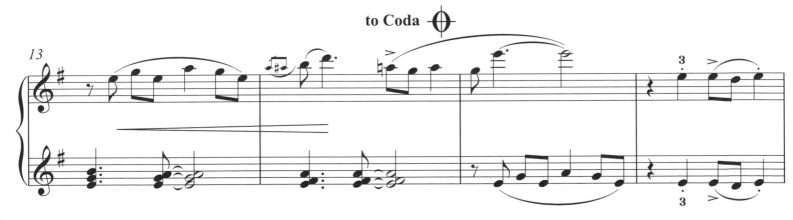

D.S. al coda

CODA

Happy Times

Christopher Norton

Happy Times

Christopher Norton

Cheerfully ♩ = 152

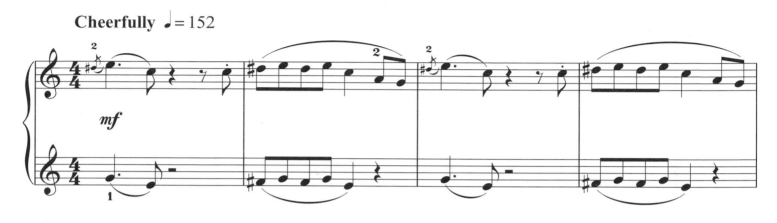

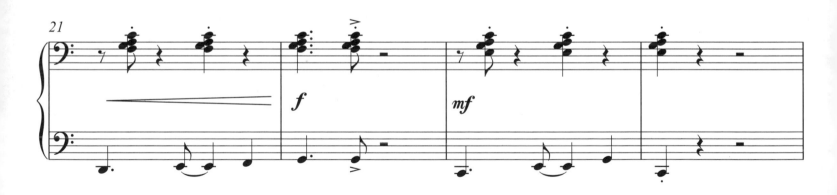

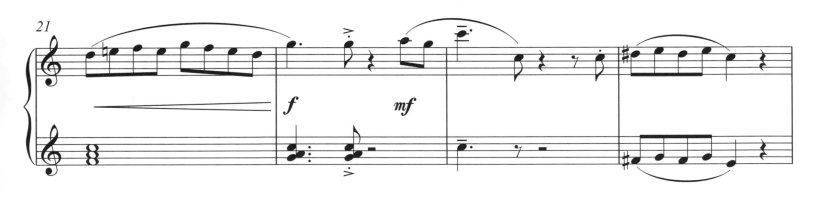

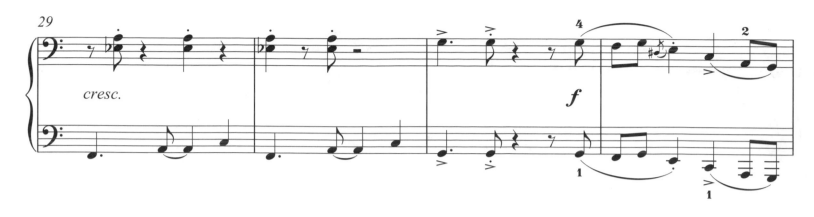

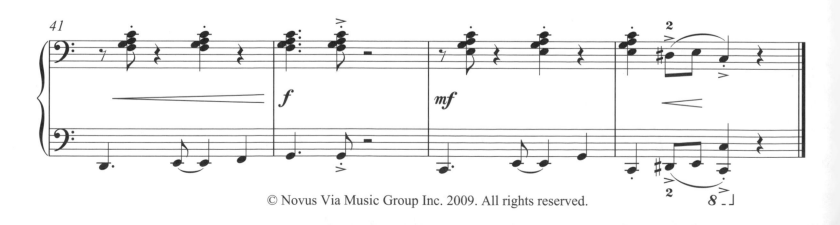

Starlight

Christopher Norton

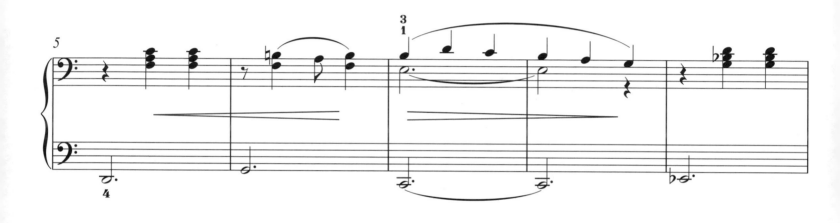

PIANO SOLO

Starlight

Christopher Norton

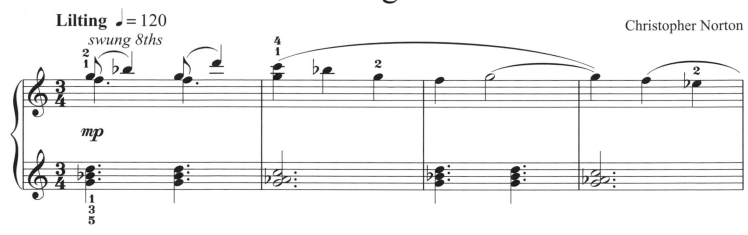

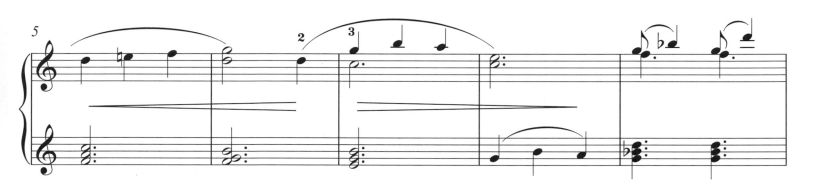

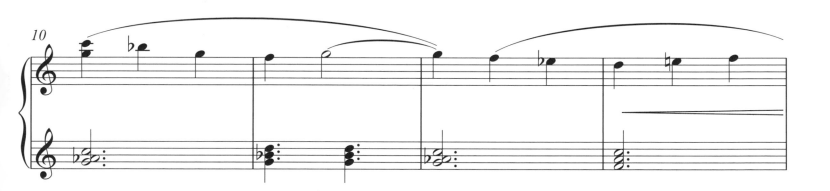

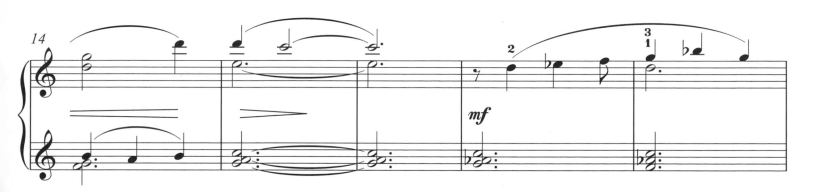

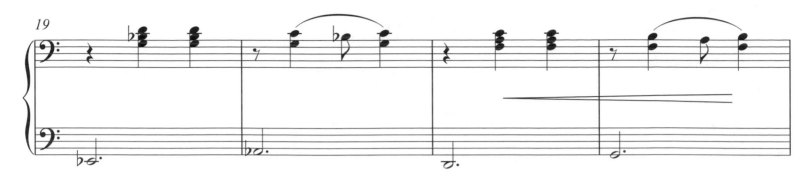

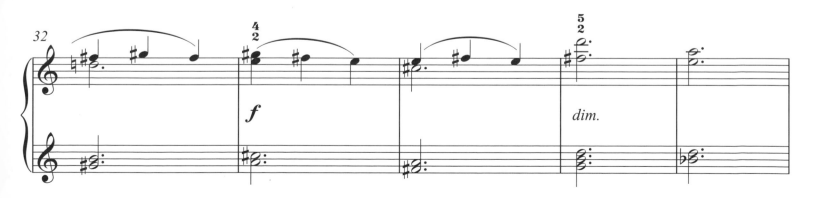

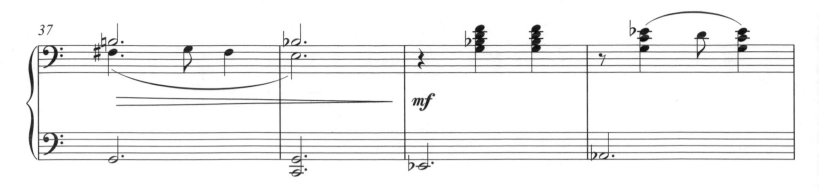

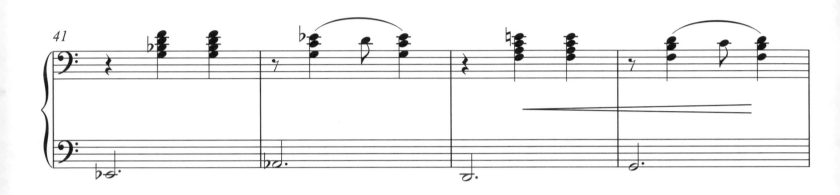

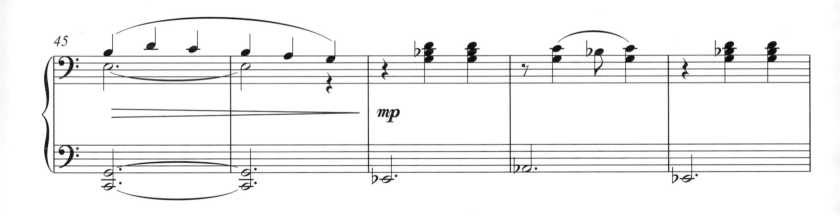

Slowing

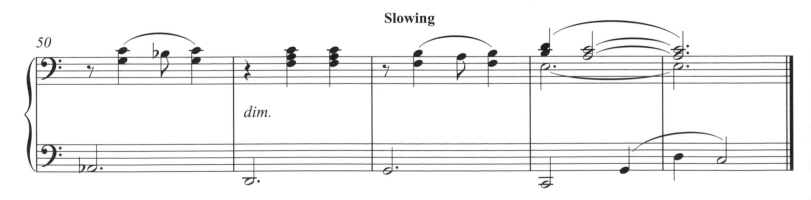

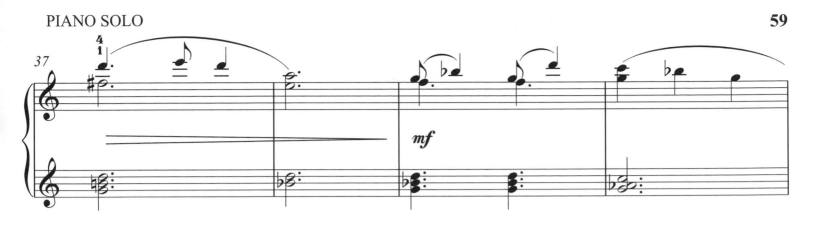

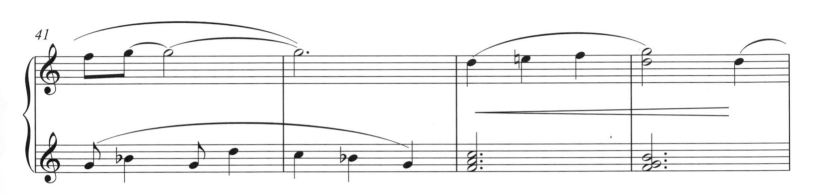

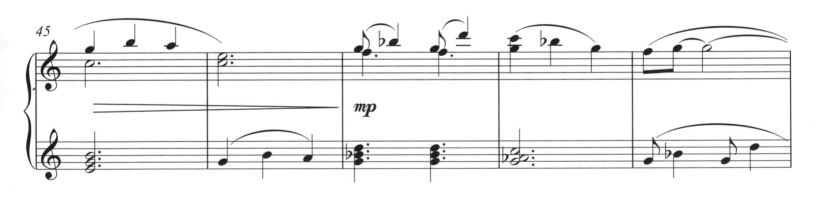

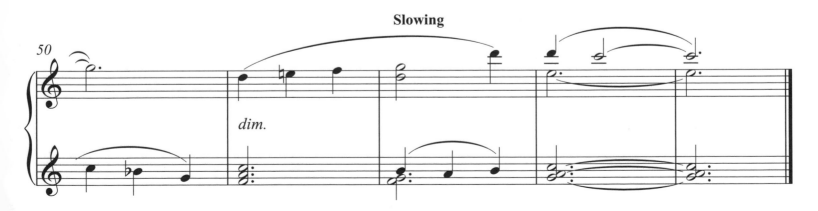

The Bigger Picture

Christopher Norton

PIANO SOLO

The Bigger Picture

Christopher Norton

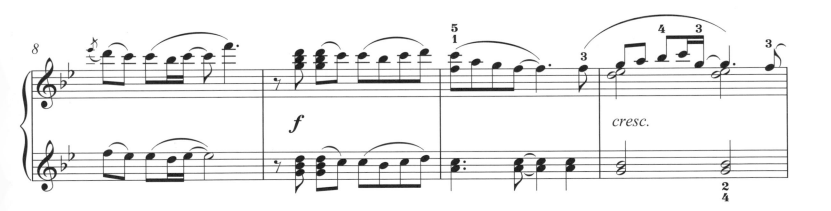

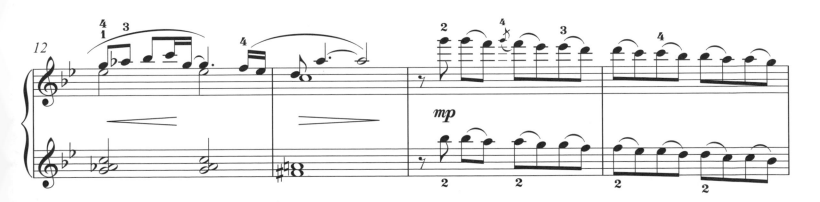

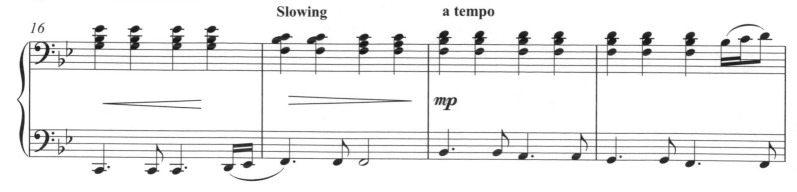

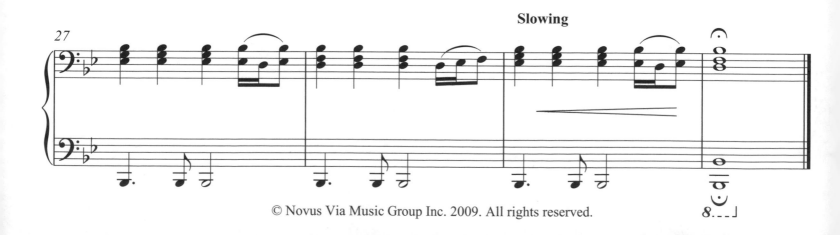

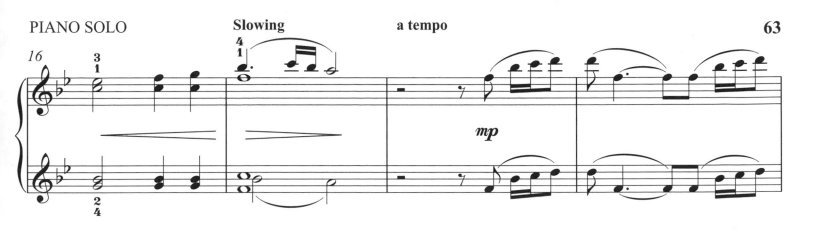

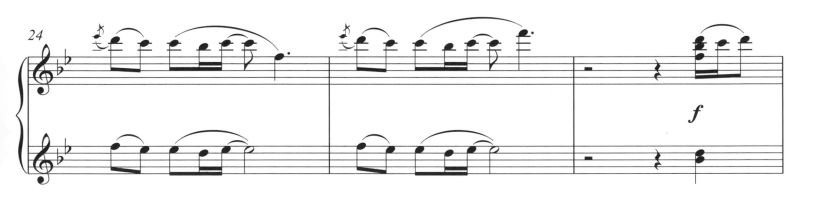

Seaside Town

Christopher Norton

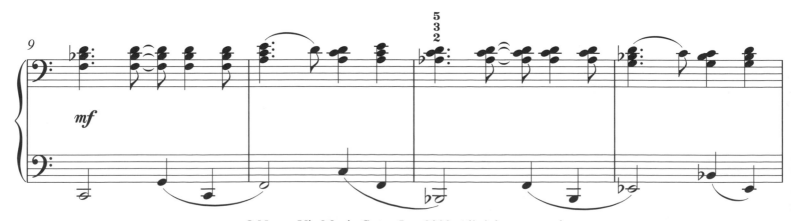

Seaside Town

Christopher Norton

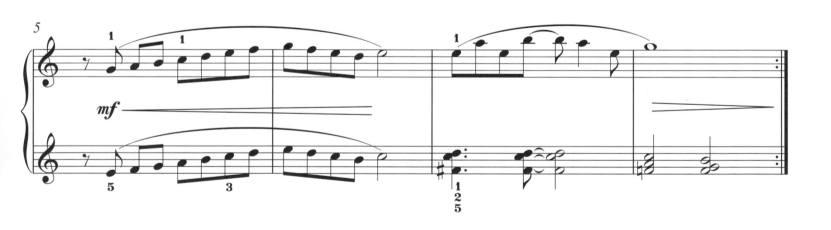

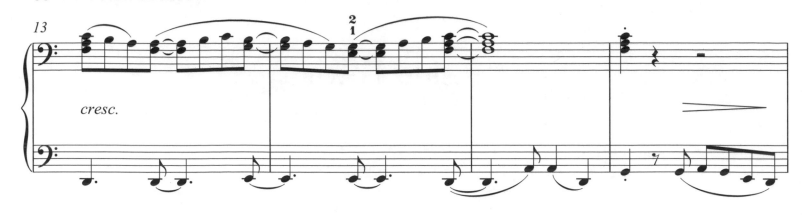

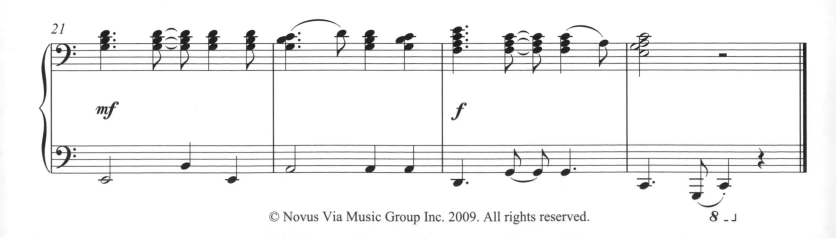

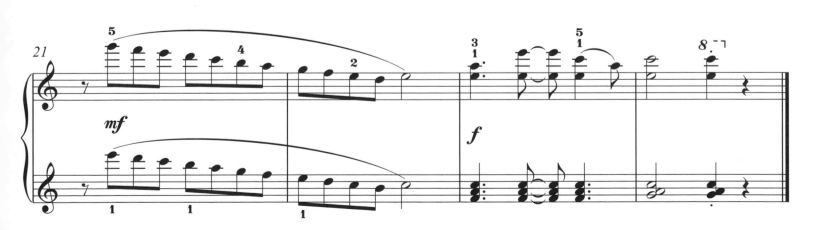

Basket Weaver

Christopher Norton

Basket Weaver

Christopher Norton

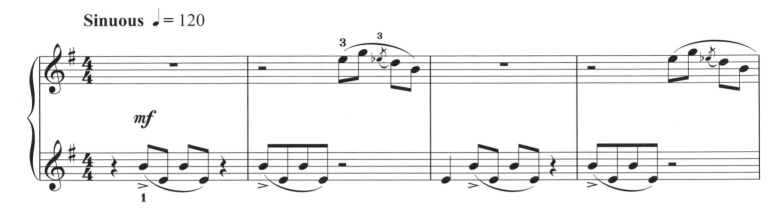

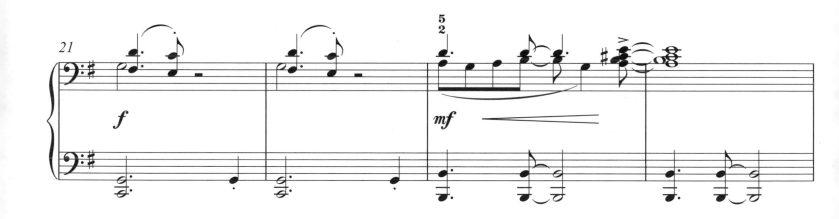

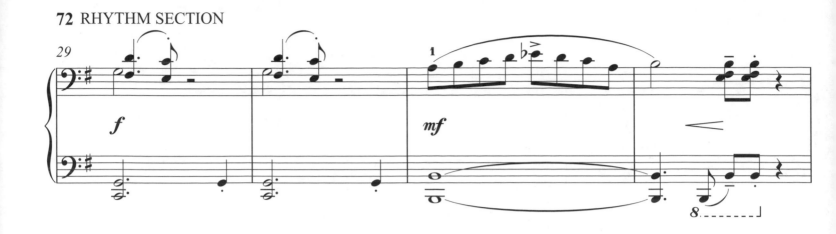

LEVEL 6 REPERTOIRE
Glossary

Backbeat....... The most common rhythm in rock music. There is an emphasis on beats 2 and 4 in a 4-beat bar, usually accented by the drums. Examples include: *The Bigger Picture*

Beguine........ A popular dance from the Caribbean, similar to a slow type of rhumba. It features flowing, sensuous melodies. Examples include: *Seaside Town*

Blues........... One of the basic forms of pop music, based on a combination of 19th century African and American song forms. There are many different types. Most feature *blue notes* (notes sung or played below pitch) and often use chords I, IV and V. Examples include: *Clean Sweep*

Blues shuffle .. A characteristic blues rhythm, based on a loose triplet feel in which the second note of the triplet is left out. There is often a strong bass. Examples include: *Shuffleboard* (APP 1)

Bolero.......... Refers to several types of Latin dance, usually slow and accompanied by castanets and acoustic guitar. Examples include: *Basket Weaver*

Boogie......... Often found in rock and country music. The left hand plays a pattern of 5ths and 6ths while the right hand plays simple, bluesy licks. Examples include: *Heavy Footed, Fireman's Boogie*

Bossa nova .... A form of Brazilian music, based on the samba, but with more lush, jazz-inflected harmonies. Examples include: *Seaside Town*

Call and........ A style of singing in which the
response   melodic phrase sung by one singer is "answered" by another. The second phrase often answers a "question" from, or "comments" on the first. Examples include: *Breaking Rocks* (APP 2)

Calypso........ A popular song form from the Caribbean island of Trinidad, using a variety of acoustic guitars and percussion instruments, particularly claves, shaker, and bongos. Examples include: *Happy Times*

Cha cha........ A Cuban dance form, with a characteristic accent on the 4th beat, ending "[rest] cha cha cha". Examples include: *Latin Promenade*

Chick Corea ... A style that combines many jazz,
style   pop, and even classical elements in a free way. Examples include: *Subdivided*

Country .... A type of pop ballad with added
ballad   country elements, especially grace notes. Examples include: *Out on the Plain*

8-beat ballad... A slow to medium tempo sentimental popular song with 8 straight 8th notes per measure. Examples include: *Bowling Green*

8-beat rock .... A staple rock 'n' roll rhythmic pattern with 8 eighth notes in every bar, and strong accents on beats 2 and 4. The accents are usually emphasized by the drums. Examples include: *On the Crest* (APP 7)

Gospel .... Religious music whose lyrics express spiritual belief. There are several types, often featuring a richly ornamented solo melody, accompanied by full harmonies. Examples include: *Summer Sunday Afternoon*

Habanera ...... A Cuban dance style, characterized by the rhythmic pattern: Examples include: *Latin Promenade*

Hoedown ...... A type of square-dance, accompanied by fiddle or banjo. It often has a feeling of 2 in a bar. Examples include: *Fiddle Tune*

Jazz .... An American art form, combining African and European elements. The definition of jazz has expanded to include almost all types of popular music. It always features some improvisation.

Jazz ballad..... A short, slow song for piano or with piano accompaniment, often along with bass and drums. It featues rich jazz harmonies. Examples include: *Summer Sunday Afternoon*

Jazz waltz...... A relaxed swing style in 3/4 time. Examples include: *Autumn Stroll, Starlight*

Latin ballad.... A pop ballad with Latin genre influences. It is often accompanied by acoustic guitar. Examples include: *To the Stars*

Latin 8-beat.... Smooth, medium tempo popular
pop   songs with Latin rhythms. Examples include: *The Knights Prepare, Basket Weaver*

New age .... A peaceful, relaxing musical style, featuring consonant, slow-moving, repetitive chord progressions. Examples include: *Timeless*

Pop ballad ..... A slow love song found in nearly all genres of popular music, with many variations. The lyrics usually concern romance. Examples include: *Tragedy*

Pop power ..... Popularised in the 1980s, these
ballad   medium tempo ballads feature a big drum sound and heartfelt (some say "over the top") vocals. Examples include: *The Bigger Picture*

Reggae......... A music style from Jamaica, with elements of calypso, and rhythm and blues. Usually somewhat slow with strong offbeats. Examples include: *Jamaican Market* (APP 3)

Rhumba........ A dance from South America with syncopated right hand chords played over a steady bass part. Examples include: *To the Stars*

Rhythm .... A style of music that combines
and blues   blues, jazz, and gospel, characterized by strong off-beats and vocal improvisation. Examples include: *Clean Sweep, Happy Times*

Shuffle......... Based on a style of tap dance where the dancer, wearing soft-soled shoes, "shuffles" their feet in a swung 8ths rhythm. Examples include: *A Light Touch*

16-beat........ A gentle song style characterized
ballad   by continuous 16th notes in the accompaniment, often provided by the hi-hat cymbal. Examples include: *At Dusk* (APP 7)

Soul .... An African-American style combining gospel and rhythm and blues.

Swing.......... An uptempo dance style, usually featuring swung 8ths. Examples include: *Summer Sunday Afternoon*

Swung 8ths .... 8th notes that are notated in equal pairs, but played in a gentle triplet rhythm:

Tango .... A dance originating in Argentina. It is rhythmically strict and often has a snare roll on beat 4. Examples include: *Boxed In*

Walking bass .. A bass style which has quarter notes on every beat, "walking" in scale and chord patterns. Examples include: *Taking Things in Stride* (APP 5)

Waltz........... A dance in 3/4 time, often played with an accent on beat 1. Examples include: *A Delicate Hue, On the Lake, Lonely Waltz* (APP 7)